50 Low Waste Cooking Recipes for Home

By: Kelly Johnson

Table of Contents

- Vegetable Scraps Broth
- Stale Bread Panzanella
- Potato Peel Chips
- Broccoli Stem Slaw
- Carrot Top Pesto
- Citrus Peel Marmalade
- Leftover Rice Stir-Fry
- Beet Greens Salad
- Onion Skin Vegetable Stock
- Herb Stems Chimichurri
- Squash Seed Granola
- Radish Top Soup
- Eggshell Fertilizer Omelette
- Pumpkin Rind Curry
- Lemon Zest Hummus
- Corn Cob Chowder
- Avocado Pit Infused Oil
- Garlic Scape Stir-Fry
- Cauliflower Leaves Gratin
- Fruit Scrap Smoothie
- Apple Core Cider
- Leftover Quinoa Salad
- Green Onion Garnish
- Mushroom Stems Risotto
- Cabbage Core Slaw
- Tomato Leaf Pasta
- Pickled Vegetable Scraps
- Watermelon Rind Pickles
- Used Coffee Grounds Cookies
- Cucumber Peel Salad
- Zucchini Blossom Fritters
- Pea Pod Soup
- Sweet Potato Skin Tacos
- Broccoli Leaf Chips
- Leftover Meat Pie

- Citrus Juice Marinade
- Herb-Infused Vinegar
- Date Pit Smoothie
- Leftover Pasta Bake
- Skillet Vegetable Hash
- Pickled Beet Greens
- Apple Peels Tea
- Savory Oatmeal with Scraps
- Cauliflower Stem Stew
- Spent Grain Bread
- Shrimp Shell Stock
- Rice Water Fertilizer
- Nut Milk Pulp Granola
- Salad Dressing from Scraps
- Baked Vegetable Scrap Frittata

Vegetable Scraps Broth

Ingredients:

- 4 cups vegetable scraps (onion peels, carrot tops, celery leaves, etc.)
- 10 cups water
- 2 cloves garlic, smashed
- 1 bay leaf
- Salt and pepper (to taste)
- Fresh herbs (optional, like thyme or parsley)

Instructions:

1. **Combine Ingredients**: In a large pot, combine vegetable scraps, water, garlic, bay leaf, salt, and pepper.
2. **Simmer**: Bring to a boil, then reduce heat and let simmer for 30-60 minutes.
3. **Strain**: Strain the broth through a fine mesh sieve, discarding the solids.
4. **Store**: Use immediately or store in the fridge for up to a week or freeze for later use.

Stale Bread Panzanella

Ingredients:

- 4 cups stale bread, cubed
- 2 cups ripe tomatoes, chopped
- 1 cucumber, diced
- 1/2 red onion, thinly sliced
- 1/4 cup fresh basil, torn
- 1/4 cup olive oil
- 2 tablespoons red wine vinegar
- Salt and pepper (to taste)

Instructions:

1. **Toast Bread**: Preheat oven to 375°F (190°C). Spread bread cubes on a baking sheet and toast until golden, about 10-15 minutes.
2. **Combine Vegetables**: In a large bowl, mix tomatoes, cucumber, red onion, and basil.
3. **Add Bread**: Add toasted bread cubes to the vegetable mixture.
4. **Dress Salad**: Drizzle with olive oil and red wine vinegar. Season with salt and pepper, then toss to combine.
5. **Serve**: Let sit for 15 minutes to allow flavors to meld before serving.

Potato Peel Chips

Ingredients:

- Potato peels from 4-6 potatoes
- 2 tablespoons olive oil
- Salt and seasoning (like paprika or garlic powder, optional)

Instructions:

1. **Preheat Oven**: Preheat to 400°F (200°C).
2. **Prepare Peels**: Rinse potato peels and pat dry. Toss with olive oil and seasonings.
3. **Bake**: Spread peels in a single layer on a baking sheet. Bake for 15-20 minutes until crispy, flipping halfway through.
4. **Serve**: Enjoy as a crunchy snack!

Broccoli Stem Slaw

Ingredients:

- 2 cups broccoli stems, peeled and julienned
- 1 carrot, grated
- 1/4 cup red cabbage, shredded
- 1/4 cup apple cider vinegar
- 2 tablespoons olive oil
- 1 tablespoon honey (or maple syrup)
- Salt and pepper (to taste)

Instructions:

1. **Prepare Slaw**: In a bowl, combine broccoli stems, carrot, and red cabbage.
2. **Make Dressing**: In a separate bowl, whisk together apple cider vinegar, olive oil, honey, salt, and pepper.
3. **Combine**: Pour dressing over the slaw and toss to coat.
4. **Serve**: Let sit for 10 minutes before serving to allow flavors to meld.

Carrot Top Pesto

Ingredients:

- 2 cups carrot tops, chopped (leaves only)
- 1/2 cup nuts (like walnuts or pine nuts)
- 2 cloves garlic
- 1/2 cup olive oil
- 1/4 cup grated Parmesan cheese
- Salt and pepper (to taste)

Instructions:

1. **Blend Ingredients**: In a food processor, combine carrot tops, nuts, garlic, and Parmesan. Pulse to combine.
2. **Add Oil**: With the processor running, slowly drizzle in olive oil until smooth.
3. **Season**: Season with salt and pepper to taste.
4. **Serve**: Use as a pasta sauce, spread, or dip.

Citrus Peel Marmalade

Ingredients:

- Peels from 4 citrus fruits (like oranges or lemons)
- 2 cups water
- 2 cups sugar
- 1/4 cup lemon juice

Instructions:

1. **Prepare Peels**: Remove the white pith from citrus peels and cut into thin strips.
2. **Cook Peels**: In a saucepan, combine peels and water. Bring to a boil, then simmer for about 15 minutes.
3. **Add Sugar**: Stir in sugar and lemon juice, cooking until the mixture thickens, about 20-30 minutes.
4. **Jar and Store**: Pour into sterilized jars and let cool before sealing.

Leftover Rice Stir-Fry

Ingredients:

- 2 cups leftover rice
- 1 cup mixed vegetables (fresh or frozen)
- 2 eggs, beaten (optional)
- 2 tablespoons soy sauce
- 1 tablespoon sesame oil
- Green onions, chopped (for garnish)

Instructions:

1. **Sauté Vegetables**: In a skillet, heat sesame oil over medium heat. Add mixed vegetables and sauté until tender.
2. **Add Rice**: Stir in leftover rice and soy sauce, cooking until heated through.
3. **Add Eggs**: If using, push rice to one side of the skillet and scramble the beaten eggs on the other side. Mix everything together.
4. **Serve**: Garnish with green onions before serving.

Beet Greens Salad

Ingredients:

- 2 cups beet greens, washed and chopped
- 1/2 cup cooked beets, diced
- 1/4 cup feta cheese, crumbled
- 1/4 cup walnuts, toasted
- 2 tablespoons olive oil
- 1 tablespoon balsamic vinegar
- Salt and pepper (to taste)

Instructions:

1. **Combine Ingredients**: In a large bowl, mix beet greens, diced beets, feta, and walnuts.
2. **Make Dressing**: In a small bowl, whisk together olive oil, balsamic vinegar, salt, and pepper.
3. **Dress Salad**: Drizzle dressing over the salad and toss to combine.
4. **Serve**: Enjoy fresh!

These recipes help you make the most of your ingredients and reduce waste while enjoying delicious meals!

Onion Skin Vegetable Stock

Ingredients:

- 2 cups onion skins (from yellow or red onions)
- 10 cups water
- 2-3 garlic cloves, smashed
- 2-3 carrots, roughly chopped
- 2-3 celery stalks, roughly chopped
- 1 bay leaf
- Salt and pepper (to taste)

Instructions:

1. **Combine Ingredients**: In a large pot, add onion skins, water, garlic, carrots, celery, bay leaf, salt, and pepper.
2. **Simmer**: Bring to a boil, then reduce heat and let simmer for 30-45 minutes.
3. **Strain**: Strain the stock through a fine mesh sieve, discarding the solids.
4. **Store**: Use immediately or store in the fridge for up to a week, or freeze for later use.

Herb Stems Chimichurri

Ingredients:

- 1 cup mixed herb stems (parsley, cilantro, dill, etc.)
- 3 cloves garlic
- 1/2 cup olive oil
- 2 tablespoons red wine vinegar
- 1 teaspoon red pepper flakes
- Salt and pepper (to taste)

Instructions:

1. **Blend Ingredients**: In a food processor, combine herb stems, garlic, olive oil, red wine vinegar, red pepper flakes, salt, and pepper.
2. **Pulse**: Pulse until the mixture is finely chopped but still has some texture.
3. **Serve**: Use as a sauce for grilled meats, vegetables, or as a dressing for salads.

Squash Seed Granola

Ingredients:

- 1 cup squash seeds, cleaned and dried
- 2 cups oats
- 1/2 cup nuts (such as almonds or walnuts)
- 1/2 cup honey or maple syrup
- 1/4 cup olive oil
- 1 teaspoon vanilla extract
- 1 teaspoon cinnamon
- A pinch of salt

Instructions:

1. **Preheat Oven**: Preheat to 350°F (175°C).
2. **Mix Ingredients**: In a large bowl, combine squash seeds, oats, nuts, honey, olive oil, vanilla, cinnamon, and salt.
3. **Spread on Baking Sheet**: Spread the mixture evenly on a baking sheet.
4. **Bake**: Bake for 20-25 minutes, stirring halfway through, until golden brown.
5. **Cool and Store**: Let cool before storing in an airtight container.

Radish Top Soup

Ingredients:

- 2 cups radish tops, washed and chopped
- 1 onion, chopped
- 2 cloves garlic, minced
- 4 cups vegetable broth
- 1 medium potato, diced
- Salt and pepper (to taste)
- Olive oil

Instructions:

1. **Sauté Aromatics**: In a pot, heat olive oil over medium heat. Add onion and garlic, cooking until softened.
2. **Add Ingredients**: Stir in radish tops, potato, and vegetable broth. Bring to a boil.
3. **Simmer**: Reduce heat and let simmer for about 20 minutes until potatoes are tender.
4. **Blend**: Use an immersion blender or transfer to a blender to purée until smooth.
5. **Season and Serve**: Season with salt and pepper, and serve warm.

Eggshell Fertilizer Omelette

Ingredients:

- 2-3 eggs
- 2 tablespoons crushed eggshells (rinsed and dried)
- 1/4 cup milk
- Salt and pepper (to taste)
- 1/4 cup cheese (optional)
- Fresh herbs (for garnish)

Instructions:

1. **Prepare Eggshells**: Crush rinsed and dried eggshells into small pieces or a powder.
2. **Beat Eggs**: In a bowl, whisk together eggs, crushed eggshells, milk, salt, and pepper.
3. **Cook Omelette**: Heat a non-stick skillet over medium heat and pour in the egg mixture. Cook until the edges begin to set.
4. **Add Cheese**: If using, sprinkle cheese on one half and fold the omelette.
5. **Serve**: Garnish with fresh herbs before serving.

Pumpkin Rind Curry

Ingredients:

- 2 cups pumpkin rind, peeled and chopped
- 1 onion, chopped
- 2 cloves garlic, minced
- 1 tablespoon curry powder
- 1 can (14 oz) coconut milk
- 1 cup vegetable broth
- Salt and pepper (to taste)
- Olive oil
- Fresh cilantro (for garnish)

Instructions:

1. **Sauté Aromatics**: In a pot, heat olive oil over medium heat. Add onion and garlic, cooking until softened.
2. **Add Pumpkin Rind**: Stir in pumpkin rind and curry powder, cooking for another 2-3 minutes.
3. **Add Liquids**: Pour in coconut milk and vegetable broth, bringing to a simmer.
4. **Cook Until Tender**: Simmer for about 15-20 minutes until pumpkin rind is tender.
5. **Blend and Serve**: Blend until smooth (if desired), season with salt and pepper, and garnish with cilantro.

Lemon Zest Hummus

Ingredients:

- 1 can (15 oz) chickpeas, drained and rinsed
- 1/4 cup tahini
- Juice of 1 lemon
- Zest of 1 lemon
- 2 cloves garlic
- 2 tablespoons olive oil
- Salt and pepper (to taste)
- Water (as needed)

Instructions:

1. **Blend Ingredients**: In a food processor, combine chickpeas, tahini, lemon juice, lemon zest, garlic, and olive oil.
2. **Add Water**: Blend until smooth, adding water as needed to reach desired consistency.
3. **Season**: Season with salt and pepper to taste.
4. **Serve**: Enjoy with pita chips or veggies.

Corn Cob Chowder

Ingredients:

- 2 corn cobs, kernels removed (reserve cobs)
- 4 cups vegetable broth
- 1 onion, chopped
- 2 potatoes, diced
- 1 cup milk or cream
- 2 tablespoons butter
- Salt and pepper (to taste)

Instructions:

1. **Sauté Onion**: In a pot, melt butter over medium heat. Add onion and sauté until softened.
2. **Add Corn and Potatoes**: Stir in corn kernels, corn cobs, and potatoes. Pour in vegetable broth and bring to a boil.
3. **Simmer**: Reduce heat and let simmer until potatoes are tender, about 15-20 minutes.
4. **Remove Cobs**: Remove corn cobs, then blend the chowder for a creamier texture (optional).
5. **Finish**: Stir in milk or cream, season with salt and pepper, and serve warm.

These recipes utilize every part of your ingredients and help reduce waste while creating delicious meals!

Avocado Pit Infused Oil

Ingredients:

- 1 avocado pit, cleaned and dried
- 1 cup olive oil (or other neutral oil)

Instructions:

1. **Prepare the Pit**: Cut the avocado pit into smaller pieces using a sharp knife. Be cautious while doing this.
2. **Infuse the Oil**: In a small saucepan, combine the avocado pit pieces and olive oil. Heat over low heat for about 30-45 minutes, ensuring the oil doesn't boil.
3. **Cool and Strain**: Remove from heat and let the oil cool. Strain the oil into a clean bottle, discarding the pit pieces.
4. **Store**: Use the infused oil in dressings or drizzled over dishes for a unique flavor.

Garlic Scape Stir-Fry

Ingredients:

- 1 cup garlic scapes, chopped
- 2 cups mixed vegetables (bell peppers, broccoli, snap peas, etc.)
- 1 tablespoon soy sauce
- 1 tablespoon sesame oil (or olive oil)
- Salt and pepper (to taste)

Instructions:

1. **Heat Oil**: In a large skillet or wok, heat sesame oil over medium-high heat.
2. **Sauté Garlic Scapes**: Add garlic scapes and stir-fry for about 2-3 minutes until fragrant.
3. **Add Vegetables**: Stir in mixed vegetables and cook until tender-crisp, about 5-7 minutes.
4. **Season**: Add soy sauce, salt, and pepper. Stir well to combine.
5. **Serve**: Enjoy hot as a side or over rice.

Cauliflower Leaves Gratin

Ingredients:

- 2 cups cauliflower leaves, washed and chopped
- 1 cup heavy cream (or milk)
- 1 cup grated cheese (cheddar or Gruyère)
- 1/2 cup breadcrumbs
- 2 cloves garlic, minced
- Salt and pepper (to taste)
- Olive oil

Instructions:

1. **Preheat Oven**: Preheat to 375°F (190°C).
2. **Sauté Leaves**: In a skillet, heat olive oil over medium heat. Add garlic and cauliflower leaves, sautéing until wilted.
3. **Mix Ingredients**: In a baking dish, combine sautéed leaves, heavy cream, half of the cheese, salt, and pepper.
4. **Top and Bake**: Sprinkle breadcrumbs and remaining cheese on top. Bake for 25-30 minutes until golden and bubbly.
5. **Serve**: Enjoy as a delicious side dish!

Fruit Scrap Smoothie

Ingredients:

- 1 cup fruit scraps (peels, cores, or leftover pieces)
- 1 banana
- 1 cup spinach or kale (optional)
- 1 cup yogurt or plant-based milk
- Honey or maple syrup (to taste)

Instructions:

1. **Blend Ingredients**: In a blender, combine fruit scraps, banana, spinach (if using), yogurt, and sweetener.
2. **Adjust Consistency**: Blend until smooth, adding more liquid if necessary.
3. **Serve**: Pour into glasses and enjoy immediately!

Apple Core Cider

Ingredients:

- Cores from 6-8 apples
- 4 cups water
- 1/2 cup sugar (or to taste)
- 1 cinnamon stick (optional)

Instructions:

1. **Combine Ingredients**: In a pot, combine apple cores, water, sugar, and cinnamon stick.
2. **Simmer**: Bring to a boil, then reduce heat and simmer for about 30-40 minutes.
3. **Strain**: Strain the mixture through a fine mesh sieve, discarding the solids.
4. **Serve**: Enjoy warm or chilled, garnished with a slice of apple.

Leftover Quinoa Salad

Ingredients:

- 2 cups leftover cooked quinoa
- 1 cup chopped vegetables (bell peppers, cucumbers, cherry tomatoes)
- 1/4 cup feta cheese (optional)
- 2 tablespoons olive oil
- 1 tablespoon lemon juice
- Salt and pepper (to taste)

Instructions:

1. **Combine Ingredients**: In a large bowl, mix quinoa, chopped vegetables, and feta cheese.
2. **Dress Salad**: Drizzle with olive oil and lemon juice. Season with salt and pepper.
3. **Toss and Serve**: Toss everything together and serve chilled or at room temperature.

Green Onion Garnish

Ingredients:

- Green onion tops, trimmed

Instructions:

1. **Chop**: Simply chop the green onion tops into small pieces.
2. **Use**: Sprinkle over soups, salads, stir-fries, or any dish that could use a fresh touch.

Mushroom Stems Risotto

Ingredients:

- 1 cup mushroom stems, chopped
- 1 cup Arborio rice
- 4 cups vegetable broth (warmed)
- 1 onion, chopped
- 2 cloves garlic, minced
- 1/2 cup white wine (optional)
- 1/2 cup grated Parmesan cheese
- Olive oil
- Salt and pepper (to taste)

Instructions:

1. **Sauté Aromatics**: In a pot, heat olive oil over medium heat. Add onion and garlic, cooking until softened.
2. **Add Mushroom Stems**: Stir in chopped mushroom stems and cook for another 3-4 minutes.
3. **Toast Rice**: Add Arborio rice, stirring for 1-2 minutes until slightly translucent.
4. **Add Wine**: If using, pour in white wine and let it absorb.
5. **Cook Risotto**: Gradually add warmed vegetable broth, one ladle at a time, stirring frequently until the rice is creamy and al dente.
6. **Finish**: Stir in Parmesan, season with salt and pepper, and serve warm.

These recipes make the most of your ingredients while minimizing waste and creating delicious meals!

Cabbage Core Slaw

Ingredients:

- 1 cabbage core, chopped
- 2 carrots, grated
- 1/4 cup mayonnaise (or yogurt)
- 1 tablespoon apple cider vinegar
- 1 tablespoon honey (or maple syrup)
- Salt and pepper (to taste)

Instructions:

1. **Prepare Cabbage**: Shred the cabbage core into thin strips.
2. **Mix Ingredients**: In a bowl, combine cabbage, grated carrots, mayonnaise, apple cider vinegar, and honey.
3. **Season**: Add salt and pepper to taste.
4. **Chill and Serve**: Let it chill in the fridge for at least 30 minutes before serving.

Tomato Leaf Pasta

Ingredients:

- 1 cup tomato leaves, washed and chopped (use only young leaves)
- 2 cups cooked pasta (any shape)
- 2 tablespoons olive oil
- 2 cloves garlic, minced
- 1/4 cup grated Parmesan cheese
- Salt and pepper (to taste)

Instructions:

1. **Sauté Garlic**: In a skillet, heat olive oil over medium heat. Add minced garlic and sauté for 1-2 minutes.
2. **Add Tomato Leaves**: Stir in tomato leaves and cook until wilted, about 2-3 minutes.
3. **Combine with Pasta**: Add cooked pasta to the skillet and toss to combine. Stir in Parmesan cheese, salt, and pepper.
4. **Serve**: Enjoy warm as a unique pasta dish.

Pickled Vegetable Scraps

Ingredients:

- Scraps from vegetables (carrot tops, cucumber ends, radish greens, etc.)
- 1 cup vinegar (white or apple cider)
- 1 cup water
- 2 tablespoons sugar
- 1 tablespoon salt
- Spices (such as dill, mustard seeds, or peppercorns, optional)

Instructions:

1. **Prepare Brine**: In a pot, combine vinegar, water, sugar, and salt. Bring to a boil, stirring until sugar dissolves.
2. **Pack Jars**: Place vegetable scraps in a clean jar. Add spices if desired.
3. **Add Brine**: Pour the hot brine over the scraps, ensuring they are fully submerged.
4. **Cool and Refrigerate**: Let cool to room temperature, then seal and refrigerate for at least 24 hours before using.

Watermelon Rind Pickles

Ingredients:

- 2 cups watermelon rind, peeled and cut into chunks
- 1 cup vinegar (white or apple cider)
- 1 cup sugar
- 1 cup water
- 1 teaspoon salt
- 1 teaspoon cinnamon (or other spices like ginger, cloves)

Instructions:

1. **Prepare Rind**: In a saucepan, combine watermelon rind, vinegar, sugar, water, salt, and spices.
2. **Simmer**: Bring to a boil, then reduce heat and let simmer for about 15 minutes until the rind is tender.
3. **Cool and Store**: Transfer to a jar and let cool. Refrigerate for at least 24 hours before enjoying.

Used Coffee Grounds Cookies

Ingredients:

- 1 cup all-purpose flour
- 1/2 cup used coffee grounds
- 1/2 cup butter, softened
- 1/2 cup brown sugar
- 1/4 cup granulated sugar
- 1 egg
- 1 teaspoon vanilla extract
- 1/2 teaspoon baking soda
- Pinch of salt

Instructions:

1. **Preheat Oven**: Preheat your oven to 350°F (175°C).
2. **Mix Wet Ingredients**: In a bowl, cream together butter, brown sugar, and granulated sugar. Add the egg and vanilla, mixing well.
3. **Combine Dry Ingredients**: In another bowl, whisk together flour, used coffee grounds, baking soda, and salt.
4. **Combine Mixtures**: Gradually add the dry ingredients to the wet mixture, mixing until combined.
5. **Bake Cookies**: Drop spoonfuls of dough onto a baking sheet and bake for 10-12 minutes, until edges are golden.
6. **Cool and Serve**: Let cool before enjoying!

Cucumber Peel Salad

Ingredients:

- Peels from 2 cucumbers
- 1 cup cherry tomatoes, halved
- 1/4 cup red onion, thinly sliced
- 1/4 cup feta cheese (optional)
- 2 tablespoons olive oil
- 1 tablespoon lemon juice
- Salt and pepper (to taste)

Instructions:

1. **Prepare Peels**: Use a vegetable peeler to slice cucumber peels into thin strips.
2. **Combine Ingredients**: In a bowl, mix cucumber peels, cherry tomatoes, red onion, and feta cheese.
3. **Dress Salad**: Drizzle with olive oil and lemon juice. Season with salt and pepper, then toss to combine.
4. **Serve**: Enjoy fresh as a light salad!

Zucchini Blossom Fritters

Ingredients:

- 10-12 zucchini blossoms, cleaned and stems removed
- 1 cup all-purpose flour
- 1/2 cup water (or sparkling water)
- 1 egg
- Salt and pepper (to taste)
- Olive oil (for frying)

Instructions:

1. **Prepare Batter**: In a bowl, whisk together flour, water, egg, salt, and pepper until smooth.
2. **Heat Oil**: In a skillet, heat olive oil over medium heat.
3. **Coat Blossoms**: Dip zucchini blossoms into the batter, allowing excess to drip off.
4. **Fry Fritters**: Fry in hot oil until golden brown, about 2-3 minutes per side.
5. **Drain and Serve**: Drain on paper towels and serve warm.

Pea Pod Soup

Ingredients:

- 2 cups pea pods, strings removed
- 1 onion, chopped
- 2 cups vegetable broth
- 1 cup cream (or milk)
- Salt and pepper (to taste)
- Olive oil

Instructions:

1. **Sauté Onion**: In a pot, heat olive oil over medium heat. Add onion and sauté until softened.
2. **Add Pea Pods**: Stir in pea pods and cook for about 2-3 minutes.
3. **Add Broth**: Pour in vegetable broth and bring to a boil. Simmer for about 10 minutes.
4. **Blend**: Use an immersion blender or transfer to a blender to purée until smooth.
5. **Finish**: Stir in cream, season with salt and pepper, and serve warm.

These recipes help you minimize waste while enjoying delicious and creative dishes!

Sweet Potato Skin Tacos

Ingredients:

- Skins from 2 large sweet potatoes
- 1 cup black beans (canned or cooked)
- 1/2 cup corn (canned or frozen)
- 1 avocado, diced
- 1/4 cup salsa
- 1 teaspoon cumin
- Salt and pepper (to taste)
- Fresh cilantro (for garnish)

Instructions:

1. **Prepare Skins**: Preheat the oven to 400°F (200°C). Bake the sweet potatoes until tender, then scoop out the flesh and save it for another dish.
2. **Crisp Skins**: Place the skins on a baking sheet, brush with olive oil, and season with salt and pepper. Bake for another 10-15 minutes until crispy.
3. **Mix Filling**: In a bowl, combine black beans, corn, avocado, salsa, cumin, salt, and pepper.
4. **Assemble Tacos**: Fill the crispy skins with the bean mixture and garnish with cilantro.
5. **Serve**: Enjoy warm as a tasty taco alternative!

Broccoli Leaf Chips

Ingredients:

- 2 cups broccoli leaves, washed and dried
- 1 tablespoon olive oil
- Salt (to taste)
- Optional spices (like garlic powder or chili flakes)

Instructions:

1. **Preheat Oven**: Preheat the oven to 350°F (175°C).
2. **Prepare Leaves**: Tear broccoli leaves into bite-sized pieces and place them in a bowl.
3. **Toss with Oil**: Drizzle olive oil over the leaves, add salt and any spices, and toss to coat evenly.
4. **Bake**: Spread the leaves in a single layer on a baking sheet. Bake for 10-15 minutes, or until crispy.
5. **Cool and Serve**: Let cool and enjoy as a healthy snack!

Leftover Meat Pie

Ingredients:

- 2 cups leftover cooked meat (beef, chicken, etc.), chopped
- 1 cup mixed vegetables (frozen or fresh)
- 1 cup gravy or sauce
- 1 pre-made pie crust (or use puff pastry)
- 1 egg (for egg wash)

Instructions:

1. **Preheat Oven**: Preheat the oven to 375°F (190°C).
2. **Mix Filling**: In a bowl, combine leftover meat, mixed vegetables, and gravy. Season to taste.
3. **Assemble Pie**: Roll out the pie crust and fit it into a pie dish. Pour in the meat mixture, then cover with a second layer of crust. Seal the edges and cut slits for steam to escape.
4. **Brush with Egg**: Brush the top crust with beaten egg for a golden finish.
5. **Bake**: Bake for 30-40 minutes or until the crust is golden brown. Serve warm.

Citrus Juice Marinade

Ingredients:

- Juice of 2 oranges
- Juice of 1 lemon
- 1/4 cup olive oil
- 2 cloves garlic, minced
- 1 tablespoon honey (or maple syrup)
- Salt and pepper (to taste)
- Fresh herbs (like thyme or rosemary, optional)

Instructions:

1. **Combine Ingredients**: In a bowl, whisk together orange juice, lemon juice, olive oil, garlic, honey, salt, pepper, and herbs.
2. **Marinate**: Use immediately to marinate chicken, fish, or vegetables for at least 30 minutes (or longer for more flavor).
3. **Cook as Desired**: Grill, bake, or sauté your marinated ingredients and enjoy!

Herb-Infused Vinegar

Ingredients:

- 1 cup vinegar (white, apple cider, or red wine)
- 1/2 cup fresh herbs (like basil, thyme, or rosemary)
- Optional spices (like garlic or peppercorns)

Instructions:

1. **Prepare Jar**: In a clean glass jar, add fresh herbs and any optional spices.
2. **Add Vinegar**: Pour vinegar over the herbs, ensuring they are fully submerged.
3. **Infuse**: Seal the jar and let it sit in a cool, dark place for about 1-2 weeks, shaking occasionally.
4. **Strain and Store**: Strain the vinegar into another bottle and store it in a cool, dark place. Use in dressings or marinades.

Date Pit Smoothie

Ingredients:

- 1-2 date pits, cleaned and dried
- 1 banana
- 1 cup spinach (optional)
- 1 cup almond milk (or other milk)
- 1 tablespoon nut butter (optional)
- Ice cubes (if desired)

Instructions:

1. **Prepare Pits**: Blend the cleaned date pits in a high-power blender until finely ground.
2. **Combine Ingredients**: In the same blender, add banana, spinach, almond milk, nut butter, and ice cubes.
3. **Blend Smoothie**: Blend until smooth and creamy. Add more almond milk if needed to reach desired consistency.
4. **Serve**: Enjoy your nutritious smoothie!

Leftover Pasta Bake

Ingredients:

- 4 cups leftover pasta (with or without sauce)
- 1 cup marinara sauce (or your favorite sauce)
- 1 cup mozzarella cheese, shredded
- 1/2 cup grated Parmesan cheese
- Optional toppings (like breadcrumbs or herbs)

Instructions:

1. **Preheat Oven**: Preheat the oven to 350°F (175°C).
2. **Mix Ingredients**: In a baking dish, combine leftover pasta and marinara sauce. Stir in half of the mozzarella cheese.
3. **Top and Bake**: Sprinkle the remaining mozzarella and Parmesan cheese on top. Add optional toppings if desired.
4. **Bake**: Bake for 25-30 minutes, or until bubbly and golden. Serve hot.

Skillet Vegetable Hash

Ingredients:

- 2 cups assorted vegetable scraps (potato peels, bell pepper tops, etc.)
- 1 onion, chopped
- 2 cloves garlic, minced
- 1 tablespoon olive oil
- Salt and pepper (to taste)
- Optional toppings (like fried eggs or cheese)

Instructions:

1. **Heat Oil**: In a skillet, heat olive oil over medium heat.
2. **Sauté Aromatics**: Add onion and garlic, cooking until softened.
3. **Add Vegetables**: Stir in vegetable scraps and season with salt and pepper. Cook until vegetables are tender and crispy, about 10-15 minutes.
4. **Serve**: Top with fried eggs or cheese if desired, and enjoy warm.

These recipes are perfect for utilizing scraps and leftovers while creating delicious, satisfying meals!

Pickled Beet Greens

Ingredients:

- 2 cups beet greens, washed and chopped
- 1 cup vinegar (white or apple cider)
- 1 cup water
- 2 tablespoons sugar
- 1 tablespoon salt
- Optional spices (like garlic, mustard seeds, or peppercorns)

Instructions:

1. **Prepare Brine**: In a saucepan, combine vinegar, water, sugar, and salt. Bring to a boil, stirring until sugar dissolves.
2. **Pack Jar**: Place beet greens in a clean jar. Add any optional spices if desired.
3. **Add Brine**: Pour the hot brine over the greens, ensuring they are fully submerged.
4. **Cool and Refrigerate**: Let cool to room temperature, then seal and refrigerate for at least 24 hours before enjoying.

Apple Peels Tea

Ingredients:

- Peels from 2-3 apples
- 4 cups water
- Optional: cinnamon stick, honey, or lemon for flavor

Instructions:

1. **Boil Water**: In a pot, bring water to a boil.
2. **Add Apple Peels**: Add the apple peels (and cinnamon if using) to the boiling water. Reduce heat and simmer for 15-20 minutes.
3. **Strain and Serve**: Strain the tea into cups, sweetening with honey or lemon if desired. Enjoy warm!

Savory Oatmeal with Scraps

Ingredients:

- 1 cup rolled oats
- 2 cups vegetable broth or water
- 1 cup vegetable scraps (like carrot tops, onion peels, or leafy greens)
- 1 tablespoon olive oil
- Salt and pepper (to taste)
- Optional toppings (like a fried egg, cheese, or hot sauce)

Instructions:

1. **Cook Oats**: In a pot, combine oats and vegetable broth (or water). Bring to a boil, then reduce heat and simmer until oats are cooked, about 5 minutes.
2. **Add Scraps**: Stir in vegetable scraps and cook for an additional 2-3 minutes until heated through.
3. **Season**: Drizzle with olive oil, season with salt and pepper, and top with any optional toppings before serving.

Cauliflower Stem Stew

Ingredients:

- 2 cups cauliflower stems, chopped
- 1 onion, chopped
- 2 carrots, chopped
- 3 cups vegetable broth
- 1 can diced tomatoes (optional)
- 2 cloves garlic, minced
- Salt and pepper (to taste)
- Olive oil

Instructions:

1. **Sauté Vegetables**: In a pot, heat olive oil over medium heat. Add onion, garlic, and carrots, sautéing until softened.
2. **Add Cauliflower Stems**: Stir in cauliflower stems and cook for about 5 minutes.
3. **Add Liquid**: Pour in vegetable broth and diced tomatoes (if using). Bring to a boil, then reduce heat and simmer for 20-25 minutes until vegetables are tender.
4. **Blend (Optional)**: For a creamy texture, blend the stew using an immersion blender or regular blender. Season with salt and pepper to taste before serving.

Spent Grain Bread

Ingredients:

- 2 cups spent grains (from brewing)
- 2 cups all-purpose flour (or whole wheat)
- 1 packet (2 1/4 teaspoons) instant yeast
- 1 tablespoon sugar or honey
- 1 teaspoon salt
- 1 cup warm water

Instructions:

1. **Combine Ingredients**: In a bowl, mix spent grains, flour, yeast, sugar, and salt. Gradually add warm water, stirring until a dough forms.
2. **Knead**: Turn the dough onto a floured surface and knead for about 5-7 minutes until smooth.
3. **Rise**: Place the dough in a greased bowl, cover with a cloth, and let it rise for about 1 hour, or until doubled in size.
4. **Shape and Bake**: Preheat the oven to 375°F (190°C). Shape the dough into a loaf and place it in a greased loaf pan. Bake for 30-35 minutes or until golden and sounds hollow when tapped.
5. **Cool and Serve**: Let cool before slicing and enjoy!

Shrimp Shell Stock

Ingredients:

- Shells from 1 pound shrimp
- 4 cups water
- 1 onion, quartered
- 2 cloves garlic, smashed
- 1 carrot, chopped
- 1 bay leaf
- Salt and pepper (to taste)

Instructions:

1. **Combine Ingredients**: In a large pot, combine shrimp shells, water, onion, garlic, carrot, bay leaf, and salt and pepper.
2. **Simmer**: Bring to a boil, then reduce heat and simmer for 30-45 minutes.
3. **Strain**: Strain the stock through a fine mesh sieve, discarding the solids. Use immediately or store in the refrigerator or freezer for future use.

Rice Water Fertilizer

Ingredients:

- Water from rinsing rice (from 1 cup rice)

Instructions:

1. **Collect Water**: After rinsing rice, save the cloudy water instead of discarding it.
2. **Cool**: Let the rice water cool to room temperature.
3. **Use as Fertilizer**: Water your plants with the rice water to provide nutrients. It can be used immediately or stored in the fridge for a few days.

Nut Milk Pulp Granola

Ingredients:

- 1 cup nut milk pulp (from making nut milk)
- 1 cup oats
- 1/2 cup nuts (chopped)
- 1/4 cup honey or maple syrup
- 1 teaspoon vanilla extract
- 1/2 teaspoon cinnamon
- Optional add-ins (dried fruit, chocolate chips, seeds)

Instructions:

1. **Preheat Oven**: Preheat the oven to 350°F (175°C).
2. **Mix Ingredients**: In a bowl, combine nut milk pulp, oats, nuts, honey (or syrup), vanilla, and cinnamon. Stir until well combined.
3. **Spread and Bake**: Spread the mixture onto a baking sheet in an even layer. Bake for 20-25 minutes, stirring halfway through, until golden and crispy.
4. **Cool and Store**: Let cool completely before adding any optional ingredients. Store in an airtight container and enjoy as a snack or breakfast!

These recipes creatively use food scraps and leftovers while providing delicious and sustainable meals!

Salad Dressing from Scraps

Ingredients:

- Scraps from 1 lemon (peels and pith)
- 1/4 cup vinegar (white, apple cider, or red wine)
- 1/2 cup olive oil
- 1 teaspoon mustard (Dijon or whole grain)
- Salt and pepper (to taste)
- Optional: herbs (like parsley or basil stems)

Instructions:

1. **Blend Ingredients**: In a blender, combine lemon scraps, vinegar, mustard, salt, and pepper. Blend until smooth.
2. **Add Olive Oil**: With the blender running, slowly drizzle in the olive oil until emulsified.
3. **Taste and Adjust**: Taste the dressing and adjust seasoning as needed. You can also add any leftover herbs for extra flavor.
4. **Store**: Transfer to a jar and refrigerate. Shake well before using.

Baked Vegetable Scrap Frittata

Ingredients:

- 2 cups vegetable scraps (like onion tops, broccoli stems, or pepper cores)
- 6 eggs
- 1/2 cup milk (or plant-based milk)
- 1 cup cheese (cheddar, feta, or your choice), grated
- Salt and pepper (to taste)
- Olive oil

Instructions:

1. **Preheat Oven**: Preheat your oven to 375°F (190°C).
2. **Sauté Scraps**: In an oven-safe skillet, heat a drizzle of olive oil over medium heat. Add vegetable scraps and sauté until softened, about 5-7 minutes.
3. **Whisk Eggs**: In a bowl, whisk together eggs, milk, salt, and pepper.
4. **Combine and Cook**: Pour the egg mixture over the sautéed scraps, then sprinkle cheese on top. Cook on the stovetop for about 2-3 minutes until the edges start to set.
5. **Bake**: Transfer the skillet to the preheated oven and bake for 15-20 minutes, or until the frittata is fully set and golden on top.
6. **Cool and Serve**: Let cool slightly, then slice and serve warm or at room temperature.

Enjoy these delicious ways to reduce waste while savoring fresh flavors!

www.ingramcontent.com/pod-product-compliance
Lightning Source LLC
LaVergne TN
LVHW081341060526
838201LV00055B/2779